THE FABER EASY-PLAY KEYBOARD SERIES

Play Romantic PARIS

arranged for easy keyboard
by Daniel Scott

FABER MUSIC

Contents

© 1989 by Faber Music Ltd
First published in 1989 by Faber Music Ltd
3 Queen Square, London WC1N 3AU
Music drawn by Sambo Music Engraving
Cover design and typography by John Bury
Printed in England
All rights reserved

Theme from *Harold en Italie*

HECTOR BERLIOZ

© 1989 by Faber Music Ltd

This music is copyright. Photocopying is illegal.

Theme from Overture *Le Corsair*

HECTOR BERLIOZ

Theme from Overture *Le carnaval romain*

HECTOR BERLIOZ

4

Nocturne Op. 9 No. 2

FRÉDÉRIC CHOPIN

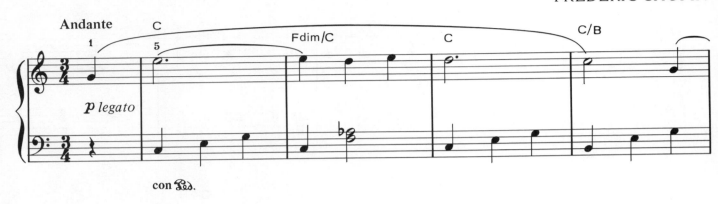

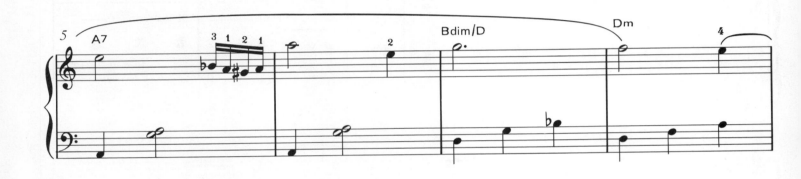

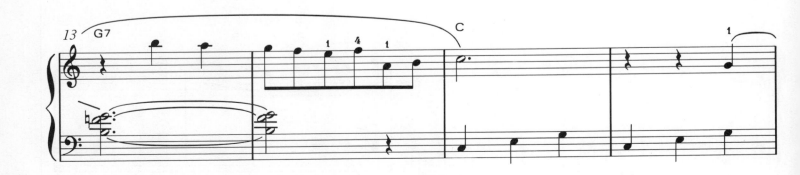

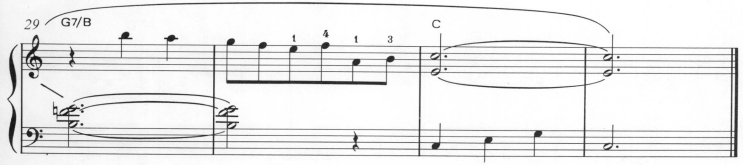

Habanera from *Carmen*

GEORGES BIZET

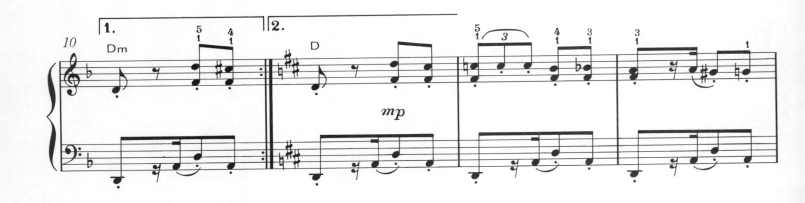

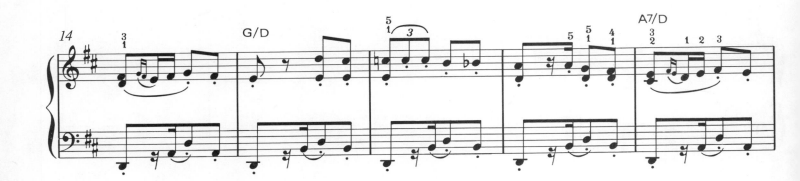

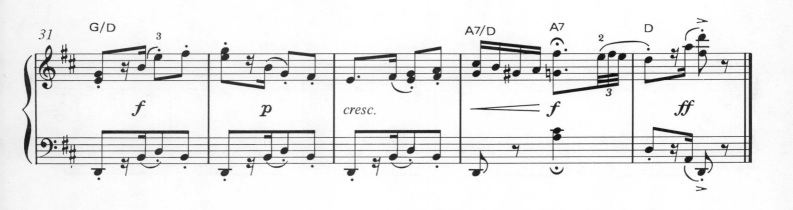

Farandole from L'Arlésienne

GEORGES BIZET

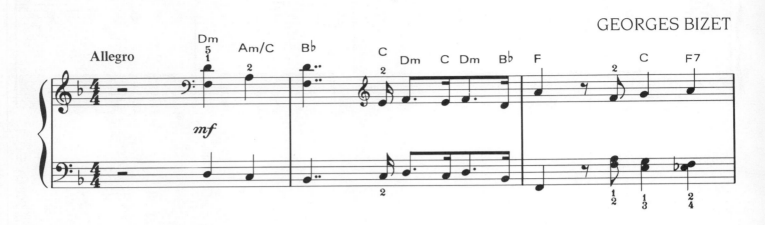

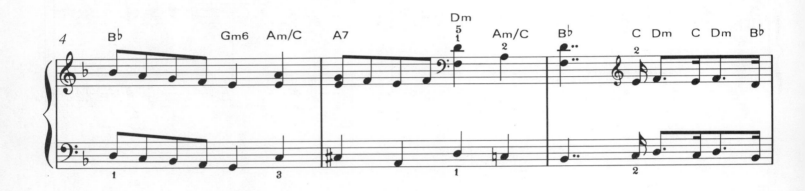

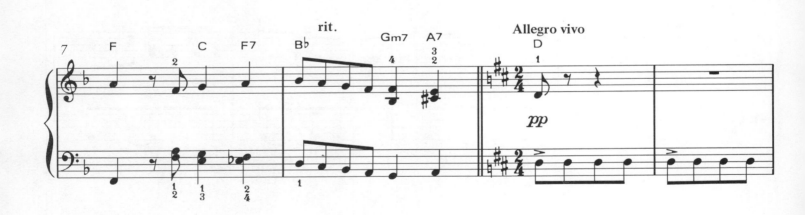

Toreador's Song from *Carmen*

GEORGES BIZET

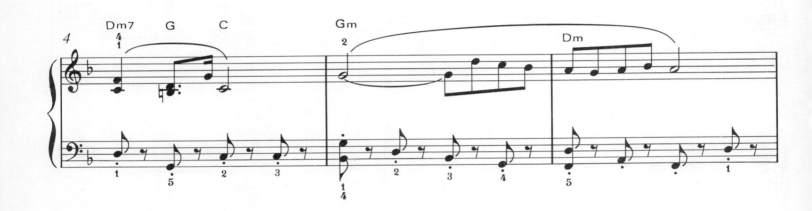

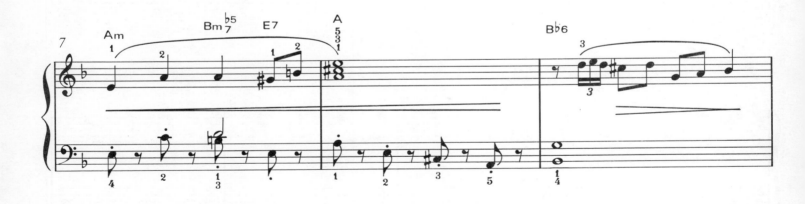

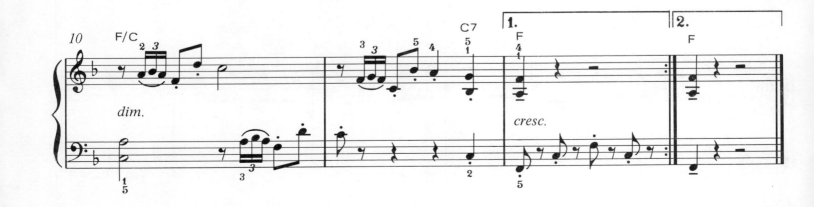

Entrée from *Giselle*

ADOLPHE ADAM

Soldiers' Chorus from *Faust*

CHARLES GOUNOD

Waltz from *Faust*

CHARLES GOUNOD

Mazurka from *Coppélia*

LÉO DELIBES

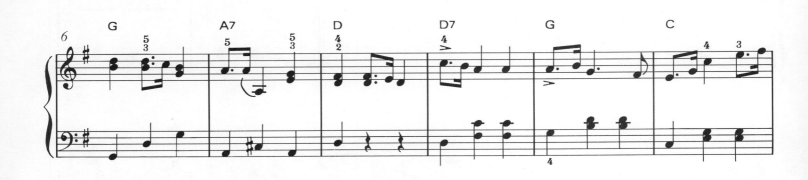

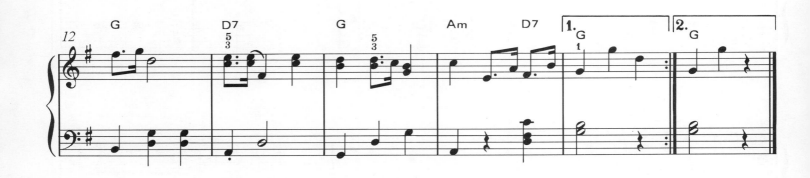

Waltz from *Coppélia*

LÉO DELIBES

Barcarolle from *Les contes d'Hoffmann*

JACQUES OFFENBACH

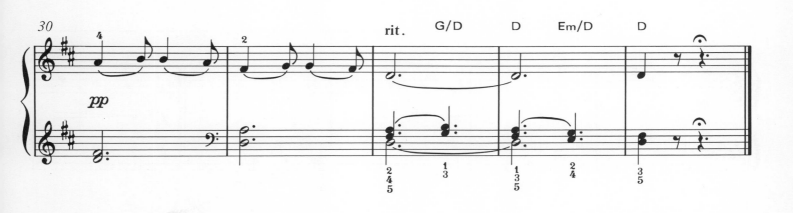

Galop from *Orphée aux enfers*

JACQUES OFFENBACH

Gendarmes' Duet from *Geneviève de Brabant*

JACQUES OFFENBACH

Meditation from *Thaïs*

JULES MASSENET

Danse macabre

CAMILLE SAINT-SAËNS

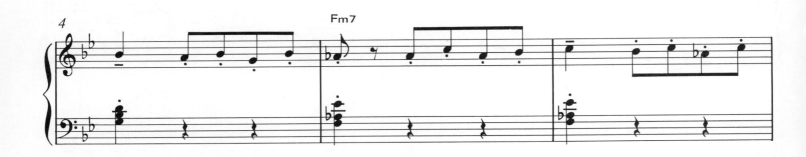

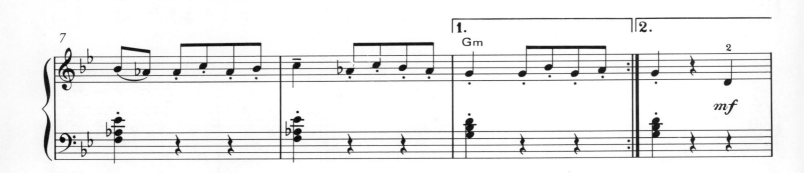

The Swan from *Le carnaval des animaux*

CAMILLE SAINT-SAËNS

Je te veux (Waltz)

ERIK SATIE

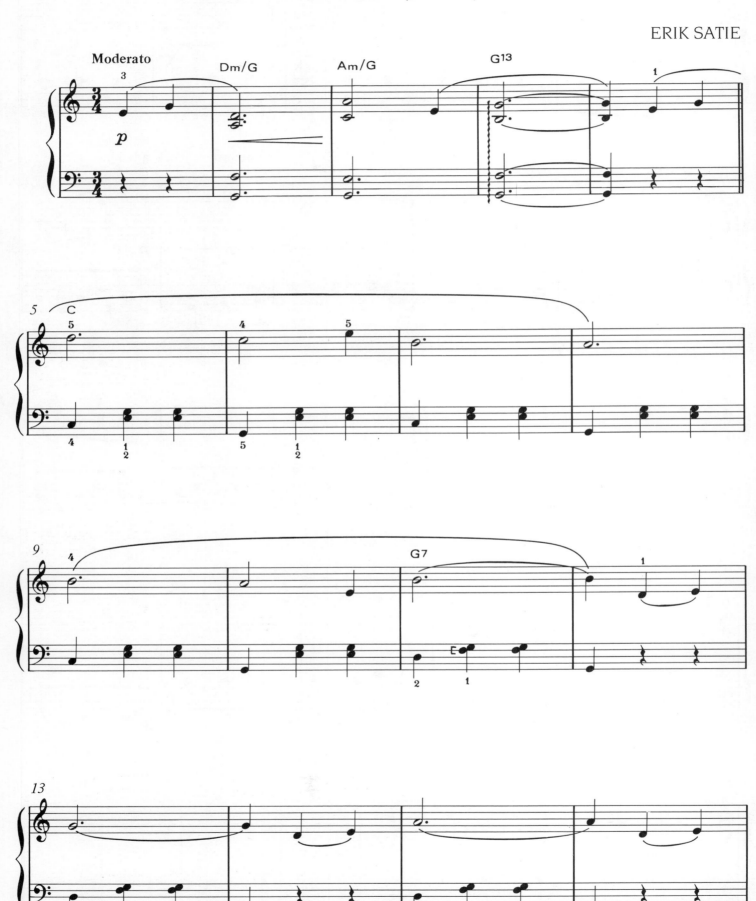

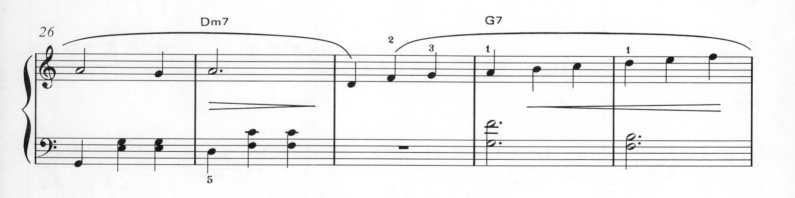
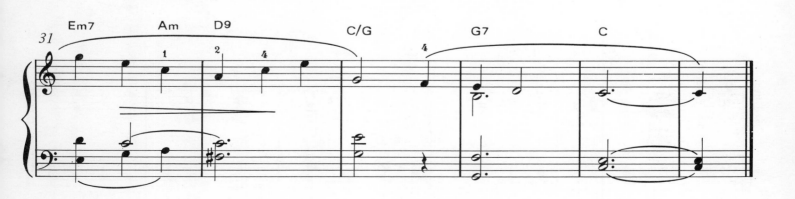

Ragtime from *Parade*

ERIK SATIE

Pavane

GABRIEL FAURÉ

Berceuse from 'Dolly' Suite

GABRIEL FAURÉ

Clair de lune

CLAUDE DEBUSSY

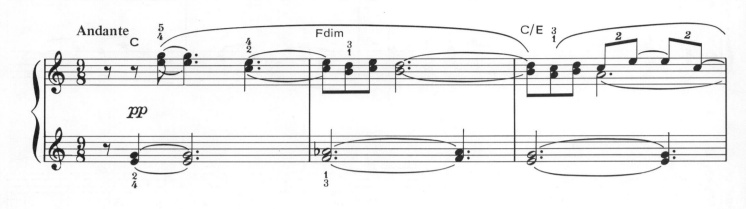

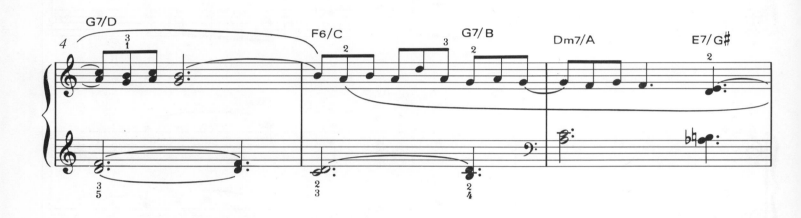

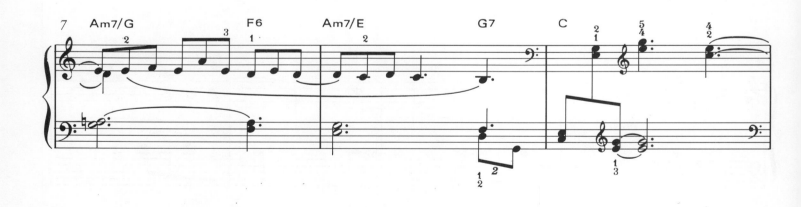

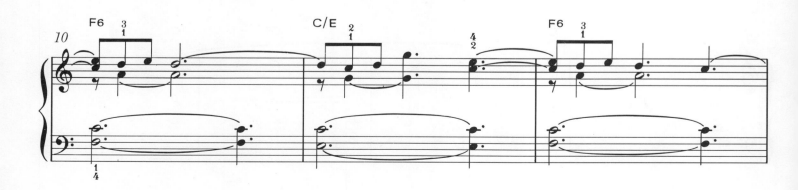

La fille aux cheveux de lin

CLAUDE DEBUSSY

Pavane

MAURICE RAVEL

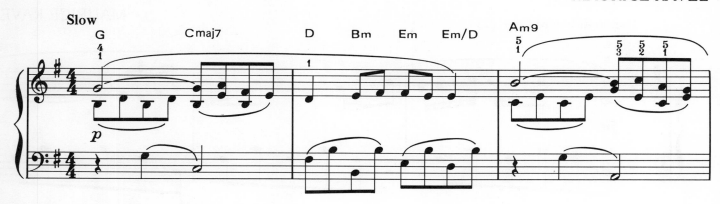

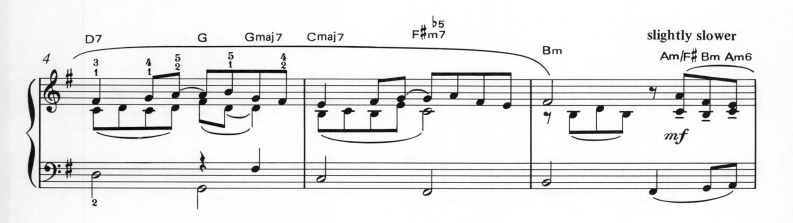

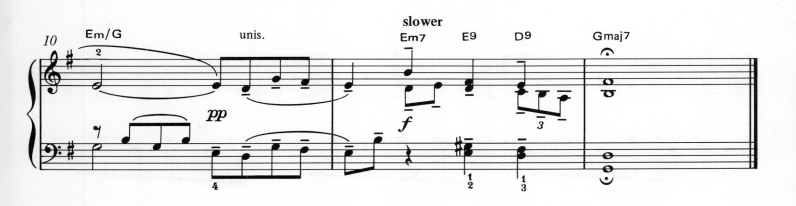

Boléro

MAURICE RAVEL